George Washington's
First Victory

by **Stephen Krensky**

illustrated by
Diane Dawson Hearn

Aladdin

New York   London   Toronto   Sydney

For all my nephews—Corey, David, Brian, Daniel, and Michael
—S. K.

To Susan Stigall, with thanks for all your support
—D. D. H.

First Aladdin Paperbacks edition January 2005

ALADDIN PAPERBACKS
An imprint of Simon & Schuster Children's Publishing Division
1230 Avenue of the Americas
New York, NY 10020

Book design by Lisa Vega
The text of this book was set in 18-Point Century Old Style BT.

Printed in the United States of America
17 19 20 18 16
0616 LAK

Krensky, Stephen.
George Washington's first victory / by Stephen Krensky ; illustrated by Diane
Dawson Hearn. —1st Aladdin Paperbacks ed.
p. cm. —(Ready-to-read stories of famous Americans)
Summary: Describes an incident in the early life of George Washington,
which provides a glimpse of his relationship with his mother.
ISBN 0-689-85942-2 (pbk) —ISBN 0-689-85943-0 (lib. ed.)
1. Washington, George, 1732-1799—Childhood and youth—Juvenile literature.
2. Presidents—United States—biography—Juvenile literature.
[1. Washington, George, 1732-1799—childhood and youth. 2. Presidents.]
I. Hearn, Diane Dawson, ill. II. Title. III. Series.

E312.66.K67 2004
973.4'1'092--dc22
2003016822

George Washington's
First Victory

Young George Washington

was almost ready for school.

He finished eating his corn bread

and brushed away a few crumbs.

His mother, Mary, sat at the head
of the table.

"George," she said,

"please come right home after

your lessons are over."

Mary Washington didn't like it
when George was away too long.
George's father, Gus,
had died a few months earlier.

George was eleven years old,

and he was now

the man of the house.

"I won't forget," said George,

standing up.

His mother nodded.

"Thank you."

George stopped for a moment.

He wanted to ask one last question.

George took a deep breath.

"What about my visit to Lawrence?"

he asked.

Lawrence was George's
big brother. He was married
and lived in a house
called Mount Vernon.
It was thirty miles away.

Lawrence wanted George

to come for a visit,

and George very much wanted to go.

"We will discuss it further,"

said his mother,

"after you get home."

"But—" George began.

His mother held up her hand.

"Remember the sixth rule:

Speak not when you

should hold your peace."

George knew all 110

Rules of Civility.

Another was, think before you speak.

So George remained silent.

As George rode the ferry

to school,

he had time to think.

Perhaps his mother worried

that if he went away,

she would go hungry.

George knew how to fish and hunt.

What if he caught a lot of food?

Would his mother feel differently?

George looked down into the water.

He knew his mother well.

No matter how much he caught,

it would never be enough.

At school George took his seat.

The first thing they practiced

was penmanship.

George wrote his name neatly

on a piece of paper.

Spelling was a bit harder for him.

He often made mistakes.

He spelled "oyl" for "oil"

and "smoak" for "smoke."

What if his spelling improved?

Would his mother

let him go then?

George shook his head no.

George's favorite subject

was arithmetic.

He liked working with numbers

and measuring things.

Why, he could measure

their whole farm

and tell his mother how big it was.

Would she let him

visit Lawrence then?

Probably not.

Such a big farm, she would say,

would need George

to stay home

to look after it.

When the students

had a break from class,

George played leapfrog

with his friends.

With his long legs,

George was able to leap pretty high.

Would his mother let him go

because he jumped higher

than anyone else?

George didn't think so.

Jumping impressed his friends,

but it would not impress his mother.

The ferry ride home

took only a few minutes.

But to George it seemed

to take forever.

He was all out of ideas

to convince his mother.

As he looked up, he saw
his mother riding across a field.
Mary Washington rode well
and cared deeply about horses.
George got an idea.

He ran to the barn

just as his mother returned.

"I'm glad to see

you are home promptly," she said.

"I have been thinking more

about visiting Lawrence," he said.

"I am sure you have," she replied.

During his visit, George explained,

he could show everyone

how much she had taught him

about riding.

"Won't they be surprised?"

said George.

His mother paused.

She had noticed that George

was a fine horseman.

Lawrence and his wife would be

very impressed with all she

had taught him.

"Very well," she said.

"You may go."

Inside his head

George let out a big hurrah!

But on the outside

he quietly said, "Thank you."

Lawrence's world was so exciting.

There would be parties and fox hunts.

Best of all, he would

spend time with Lawrence.

George was so glad

that his mother had approved.

This was the first victory

of his life.

With any luck, he thought,

it would not be his last.

This book is based on a story about George Washington. The timeline below identifies important events in his life.

1732   Born on February 22

1743   George's father, Augustus, dies

1752   George inherits Mount Vernon after the death of his brother Lawrence

1754   Sees first military action in French and Indian War

1759   Marries Martha Custis

1774   Appointed to Continental Congress

1775   Becomes Commander-in-Chief of the Continental army

1775   After several defeats, he wins the Battle of Trenton

1781   Wins final victory at Yorktown

1789   Chosen first president of the United States; serves two terms

1796   Retires to Mount Vernon

1799   Dies on December 14